DATE DUE

DEMCO 38-296

EARTHQUAKES

Karen Spies

Twenty-First Century Books

Brookfield, Connecticut

Twenty-First Century Books
A Division of The Millbrook Press
2 Old New Milford Road
Brookfield, CT 06804

Printed in the United States of America

Created and produced in association with Blackbirch Graphics, Inc.

Library of Congress Cataloging-in-Publication Data

Spies, Karen Bornemann.
    Earthquakes / Karen Spies. — 1st ed.
        p.   cm. — (When disaster strikes)
    Includes index.
    ISBN 0-8050-3096-4 (alk. paper)
    1. Earthquakes—Juvenile literature. [1. Earthquakes.] I. Title. II. Series.
QE521.3.S65   1994
363.3'495—dc20   93-38267
                                                                                        CIP
                                                                                        AC

Contents

Countdown to Catastrophe

San Francisco's Candlestick Park was filled with 58,000 fans. The third game of baseball's World Series would start in about half an hour. The weather was warm. No wind was blowing—it was a perfect night for baseball. Television broadcasters and fans alike began to count down the minutes until the first pitch.

It was 5:04 P.M. on October 17, 1989. Suddenly, the stillness was broken. The stadium began to tremble. The light towers swayed back and forth. Concrete blocks fell from the stadium balconies. Some people screamed,

Opposite:
Firemen enter a collapsed home in San Francisco, California, to search for injured people after the October 1989 quake.

Fans awaiting the start of a World Series game in Candlestick Park were terrified by the earthquake that struck in 1989.

while others ran for the exits. But most of the fans just stayed where they were. No one was sure what was happening.

One eyewitness said, "All of a sudden everyone stood up...with fear on their faces. A lot of people were sick and throwing up, from fear and from the swaying."

Al Michaels, a television announcer, yelled "We're having an earth—." Then the broadcast blacked out.

The earthquake lasted only fifteen seconds. As the shaking died down, the World Series crowd cheered. A few fans yelled, "Play ball!" No one at the game was aware of the destruction the earthquake had caused outside of Candlestick Park.

Rush hour traffic was stopped on the San Francisco-Oakland Bay Bridge. The quake had caused a section of the double-decker bridge to collapse, leaving a huge hole. A bus driver was able to save many lives by bringing his bus to a stop 8 feet (2 meters) from the hole. He said the earthquake had made him lose control of his bus and that it felt like all his tires had blown at once. But not everyone on the bridge was as fortunate. One driver didn't see what had happened and drove his car over the edge of the bridge. And a woman died when she was crushed by a piece of the falling bridge.

Another tragic situation took place in West Oakland. The double-decker Nimitz Freeway had been packed with cars. Without warning,

The October 1989 quake caused a part of the San Francisco-Oakland Bay Bridge to collapse, killing over 40 people.

a 1-mile (2-kilometer) section of the top deck fell onto the lower deck. Forty-two people were killed. Richard Reynolds, an auto mechanic who witnessed the disaster, said that many cars were flattened just like beer cans. Within minutes, nearby residents, such as William McElroy, age 52, rushed to the scene to help. He said, "We were worried that the freeway could collapse on us, but we had to reach out to the people moaning and groaning for help." McElroy heroically rescued 14 people.

Damage was also very heavy in the Marina District of San Francisco. Many of the buildings there had been built on soft, sandy soil. The violent shaking of the earthquake caused the sand to mix with groundwater, which caused liquefaction. The soil turned into a mixture like quicksand, and several of the buildings in the Marina District toppled over. Sand boils (holes in the sand) and sand volcanoes (spouts in the sand) appeared. The shaking also caused gas pipes to break, starting huge fires. Within a few

Many buildings in San Francisco's historic Marina District were destroyed by the 1989 quake.

hours, nearly 1 square mile (3 square kilometers) of the city was in flames.

In total, more than 1,300 buildings were destroyed. Another 20,000 were damaged. There were 67 deaths and nearly 4,000 injuries. At least 8,000 people were left homeless, and property damage totalled $10 billion.

The effects of the earthquake were felt a great distance from where it had begun, more than 50 miles (80 kilometers) south of San Francisco. Its epicenter (the point on the surface of the land where an earthquake begins) was in the Santa Cruz mountains. Its focus, or underground center, was under a peak called Loma Prieta, which means "the dark rolling mountain."

The quake was the largest one in the area in 37 years. It measured 7.1 on the Richter Scale. The Richter Scale is a system of numbers used to describe earthquake strength.

Three heavily populated towns near the epicenter were hit hard by the quake. More than 10,000 people lost their homes in Santa Cruz, Watsonville, and Hollister. The downtown area of Santa Cruz was destroyed and 3 people were killed when part of the Pacific Garden Mall collapsed on top of them.

The destruction could have been worse. Fortunately, interest in the World Series game had reduced traffic on the roads. More importantly,

the center of the earthquake ran directly through an area where few people lived. If the quake had hit right in downtown San Francisco, both the damage and the death toll would have been higher.

Rescuers use specially trained dogs to sniff out earthquake victims who might be buried in debris at the Pacific Garden Mall in Santa Cruz, California.

What Happens During an Earthquake?

If you are ever in an earthquake, you will feel the ground move. It may roll up and down or shake back and forth. A quake may make you feel like you are in a boat. Eleven-year-old Cornia Johnson described the World Series quake as "like being in a blender." The vibrating may last only a few seconds, or several minutes. Smaller quakes, called aftershocks, may take place for several days after a large earthquake.

During the shaking, many tall buildings sway back and forth. Pictures may fall off walls, and dishes may rattle or even fall out of cabinets. Trees will sway and roads may buckle. The earthquake may make a roaring noise or sound like thunder. The earth can split in large cracks. The ground on one side of a crack may sink lower than the other side. During an Alaskan earthquake in 1964, one side of Anchorage's Fourth Avenue dropped 11 feet (3 meters).

Earthquakes can cause damage in many ways. As the ground shakes, walls and ceilings may cave in. Falling bricks, stone, and broken glass may injure pedestrians. Entire buildings might collapse. Sometimes the people inside these buildings are killed. During the Mexico City earthquake of 1985, three of the city's hospitals partially collapsed, burying 1,200 people.

Fires resulting from a quake may cause even more damage. The violent shaking of the earth often breaks underground gas lines. A single spark can cause a huge fire or explosion. If a quake breaks water pipes in an area, firefighters may have a difficult time putting fires out.

The earth's shaking may sometimes cause landslides. Rocks and earth can slide into huge cracks that have been formed by a quake. The vibrations may also loosen the earth on cliffs. This can cause terrifying landslides that sweep away anything in their paths. After the Alaska earthquake of 1964, a 130-acre (53-hectare) section of a cliff slid down into Cook Inlet near Anchorage. The cliff swept away 75 houses.

Ruptured gas lines caused major fires to break out in San Francisco during the 1989 quake.

Earthquakes under the ocean may also cause waves known as tsunamis. As the ocean floor heaves during a quake, it creates large waves. They spread out and roll rapidly across the ocean. Boats far out at sea usually do not feel the motion, because the waves are too low and too far apart. But when a tsunami hits shore, the waves may be as high as 100 feet (30 meters).

The Ever-Changing Earth

You can see that earthquakes destroy lives and property in many ways. Within only a matter of minutes, a whole city can be totally wiped out. Homes that have stood for years can be turned into piles of splintered wood. Death can strike families without warning.

A million times a year, throughout the world, an earthquake takes place. This averages out to one earthquake every thirty seconds. These quakes are changing the face of the earth.

INSIDE OUR EARTH

The earth is made up of different layers. The center is called the core. It is about 3,200 miles (5,150 kilometers) thick and is composed of iron and nickel. The inner core is solid and the outer core is liquid.

Around the core is the mantle. It is made of solid, hot rock and is about 1,800 miles (2,900 kilometers) deep. Floating on the mantle is the crust. We live on the earth's crust. As the mantle below moves around on the fluid outer core, it cracks the crust. These cracks have broken the earth's crust into huge pieces called plates. To picture these plates, compare the earth to a hard-boiled egg with a cracked shell. Each piece of shell is similar to one of the earth's plates.

For hundreds of years, scientists have tried to understand the forces that cause earthquakes. Today, complex scientific instruments help them to measure the power of quakes. Scientists have learned that the earth beneath our feet is not solid. In certain places, continents are being torn apart, and in other areas, they are being smashed together. Even the ocean floor is always changing.

Earthquakes can cause major fissures, or cracks, in the earth. This fissure was created by the World Series quake.

Disasters and You

Earthquakes will continue to occur, as will all natural disasters, such as floods and hurricanes. People can't stop these disasters from taking place, but they can be prepared to face them. After reading this book, you will understand some of the science behind earthquakes and how they happen, and you will know what to do in case of an earthquake.

△ 13

What Causes Earthquakes?

Ancient peoples did not have scientific explanations for earthquakes. Instead, they created myths and legends to explain what they could not understand. In many early cultures, people believed that the earth was carried on the backs of animals such as oxen, frogs, or snakes. For example, some Native Americans believed that seven sea turtles held up the earth. When they moved, the earth cracked and quakes followed.

In India, people once believed that four elephants supported the earth. The elephants stood on the back of a turtle, while the turtle

Opposite:
This special effects photo simulates a powerful quake in San Francisco. Scientists can study such simulations to learn about the causes of earthquakes.

balanced on a snake. If any of these animals made even the smallest movement, the earth would tremble and cause a quake.

The ancient Greeks thought that earthquakes showed the gods' anger. A giant named Atlas had rebelled against the gods. As punishment, he had to hold up the world on his shoulders. When Atlas shrugged his shoulders, the Greeks said, an earthquake took place.

Aristotle, the Greek philosopher, was one of the first to try to explain earthquakes using logic as opposed to myth. He believed that hot air was caught in underground caves. As the hot wind blew and tried to escape, earthquakes occurred. William Shakespeare, the English writer, mentioned this idea in one of his plays, *Henry IV*.

Early scientists believed that large movements of rocks had something to do with earthquakes. But most of those scientists thought the movement was caused by underground explosions.

A Puzzling Issue

One thing that fascinated early scientists was the shape of the continents. In 1620, English scholar Sir Francis Bacon noticed how similar in shape the continents were. The coast of Europe looked as if it might match up with the North American coastline. And the curve of Central America appeared to fit the western bulge of

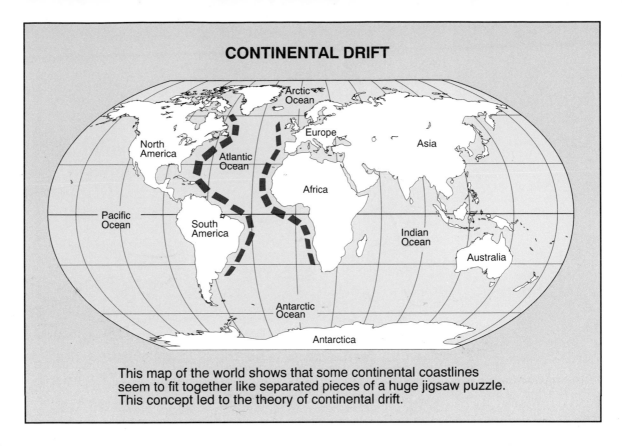

CONTINENTAL DRIFT

This map of the world shows that some continental coastlines seem to fit together like separated pieces of a huge jigsaw puzzle. This concept led to the theory of continental drift.

Africa. A French naturalist, Georges de Buffon, noticed that many similar animals and plants lived in Europe and North America. Could the continents have once been one large mass of land? Could they have broken apart millions of years ago? What powerful forces might have caused such breaks?

A German scientist, Alfred Wegener, thought he had the answers to these questions. In 1912, Wegener proposed the theory of continental drift. He suggested that about 200 million years ago, the continents were one landmass. At some point, the continents had broken off, and were floating or drifting apart.

△ 17

At first, scientists criticized Wegener's ideas. But that changed when similar fossils were found on every continent. Since prehistoric animals could not have crossed the oceans, scientists theorized that there must have once been only a single large continent.

By the 1960s, scientists had found evidence to support Wegener's theory. When they began to explore the ocean, scientists discovered a giant undersea mountain range. A crack runs through the center of most of it. Part of what makes up this mountain range is hot liquid rock, or magma. As the hot rock shifts, deep crevices are created and the magma pushes upward, forming new portions of the seafloor. As this seafloor grows, it moves the continents apart. They seem to be floating and drifting along the surface of the earth like giant rafts. This theory of continental drift led to another theory, known as plate tectonics.

Plate Tectonics

A plate is a large section of the earth's crust. Tectonics is the art or science of making things out of similar small pieces. According to scientists, seven to twelve large plates, and several smaller ones, make up the earth's crust. Plate tectonics studies the way the surface of the earth has been created from these plates.

The earth's plates are continually moving, perhaps as much as several inches (centimeters) a year. As they move, they bump and crunch against each other. They can spread apart from each other, or push against each other. Sometimes during this movement, one plate will come up over the top of another. In other places, two plates will slide along next to one another.

In all of these situations, pressure begins to build up. Imagine the tension in a stretched rubber band, and you will begin to have an idea of what the pressure build-up underground is like. At some point, the earth can't take any

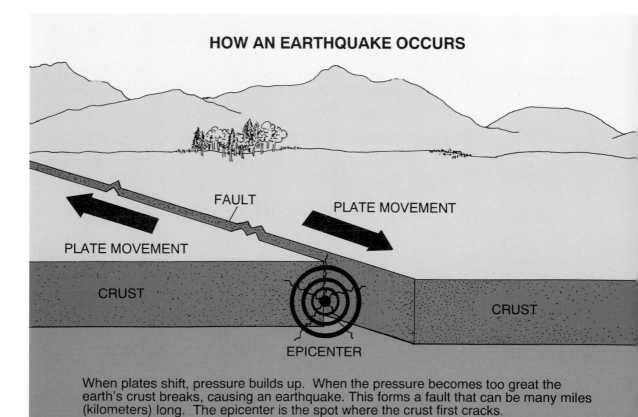

HOW AN EARTHQUAKE OCCURS

FAULT

PLATE MOVEMENT

PLATE MOVEMENT

CRUST

CRUST

EPICENTER

When plates shift, pressure builds up. When the pressure becomes too great the earth's crust breaks, causing an earthquake. This forms a fault that can be many miles (kilometers) long. The epicenter is the spot where the crust first cracks.

Opposite:
The San Andreas fault
extends more than 600 miles
(965 kilometers) through
California. This fault is the
line between the North
American Plate and the
Pacific Plate.

more pressure. It snaps, like a stretched rubber band would, when it is released. The result of this snap is an earthquake.

The area of the crust that breaks is known as a fault. Faults can be seen on the surface of the land. Any area where faults are common is known as a fault zone.

Four out of every five earthquakes take place around the edge of the Pacific Ocean. This part of the world has come to be known as the "Ring of Fire" because of the numerous volcanoes in the region. It is also an area of great seismic (earthquake) activity. Quakes result when the Pacific Plate and neighboring plates collide.

Most of North America lies on the North American Plate. But a small part of Southern California and Mexico are located on the Pacific Plate. These two plates are moving in different directions. Los Angeles is located on the Pacific Plate, which is heading toward the northwest. Scientists believe that millions of years from now, the city will actually be next to San Francisco, which is located on the North American Plate!

Other Causes of Quakes

The movement of plates causes about 95 percent of all earthquakes. But some quakes take place in the middle of a plate. One theory is that deep faults cause quakes in the middle of a

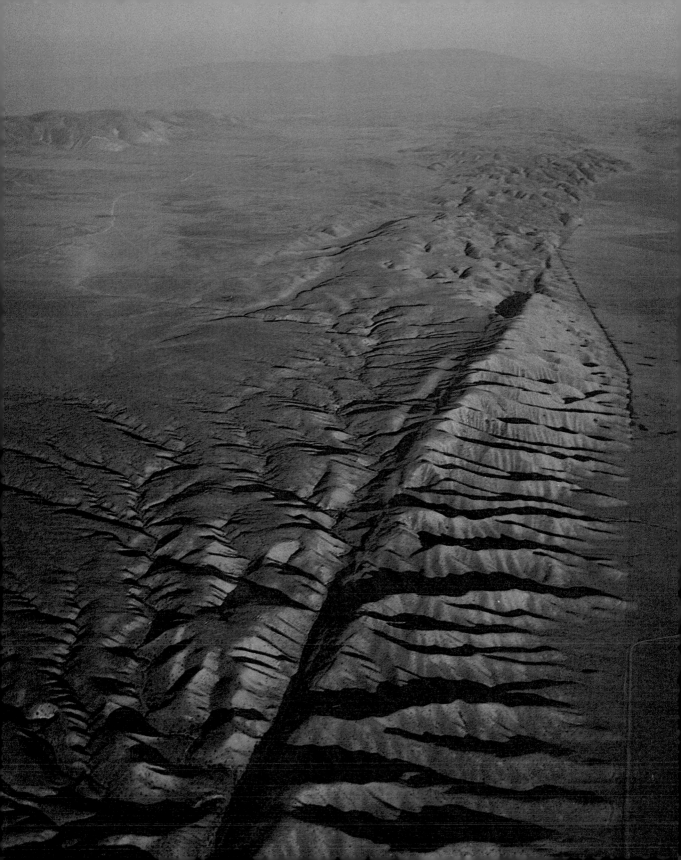

Mount St. Helens, in south-western Washington, erupting.

continent. Layers and layers of crust have been formed in long and unbroken sections. When the fault cracks, the earthquake waves move quickly through the unbroken rock. The result is a strong quake.

Volcanic eruptions can also trigger earth-quakes. During an eruption, molten rock is released from inside the earth. As it flows out of the volcano, the magma pushes upward on part of the earth surrounding the crust. This triggers quakes in the ground near the volcano.

People can also cause earthquakes. One way is by building a large dam. The lake be-hind the dam must be filled with water slowly. Otherwise, some of the water may seep into the earth and put pressure on the ground just around the dam. If pressure builds up under-ground, the earth can move suddenly and an earthquake may occur.

Measuring Quakes

To compare earthquake size, scientists use the Modified Mercalli Scale and the Richter Scale. These scales are measuring systems that use numbers to represent the actual power of an earthquake.

The Modified Mercalli Intensity Scale

The Mercalli Scale was the first tool that was used to describe earthquake intensity—how much damage a quake caused. The scale was invented in 1902 by Italian seismologist (scientist who studies earthquakes) Giuseppe Mercalli and was

EARTHQUAKES AT HOOVER DAM

Giant Hoover Dam stands more than 725 feet (221 meters) high. It was built in the 1930s to hold back the water of the mighty Colorado River. The dammed water would form Lake Mead, which would be more than 90 miles (145 kilometers) long. When the dam was completed, engineers began to fill the lake bed with water. That's when they noticed something peculiar. As the water got higher, earthquakes began to occur. The higher the water got, the more often quakes hit and the stronger they were.

The engineers worried that when the lake was full, it might crack the dam. Just as the lake began to reach its highest level, a quake measuring 5.0 on the Richter Scale hit. Luckily, the dam held.

The water in Lake Mead was kept at a steady level. Little by little, the amount and size of the quakes lessened. Today, few quakes take place there. When quakes do happen, they're so small that visitors to the dam can't feel them.

Engineers learned a lesson at Hoover Dam. Today, lakes and reservoirs are filled more slowly. This gives the surrounding earth a chance to adjust to the increased pressure of the water—without triggering earthquakes.

Dr. Charles F. Richter.

modified in 1931 by American seismologists. Scientists rate quakes on this scale using Roman numerals I to XII.

The Mercalli Scale is useful while comparing ancient and modern quakes. Scientists can study records of early quakes and then rate them.

An earthquake that can be felt only by people who are sitting on the upper floors of a building is rated a II. A quake causing pipes to crack and buildings to collapse gets a IX. The intensity of a quake can vary from place to place. Usually the Mercalli ratings are higher for areas nearer the epicenter. For example, the World Series quake measured a X in San Francisco's Marina District. Many homes there sunk into the ground and the damage was heavy. In other areas of the city, the quake rated only a VI or VII.

The Richter Scale

"Today's quake registered 4.5 on the Richter Scale."

Statements like this are often reported on the news. The Richter Scale was invented in 1935 by Dr. Charles F. Richter, an American seismologist. This scale measures the size of a quake by measuring its magnitude, or amount of energy released. It is based on information recorded on seismograms. The scale begins at

1.0 and has no upper limit. Each step on the scale stands for an earthquake that releases about ten times more energy than the step below.

An earthquake that registers 1.0 on the Richter Scale cannot be felt by people. A quake registering 2.0 still does not cause much damage. If 7.0 is reached on the scale, the power is equal to exploding 199,000 tons (180,493 metric tons) of dynamite. The 1989 World Series quake registered 7.1. A quake registering 6.0 or more is considered a major earthquake.

TURNING QUAKES "OFF" AND "ON"

At Rocky Mountain Arsenal in Denver, Colorado, chemical weapons were made from 1942 to 1982. Manufacturing these chemicals created poisonous waste products. This waste was pumped into a well that was about 2 miles (3 kilometers) deep. One month after pumping began, an earthquake hit. The quakes continued whenever waste pumping was done. But when it was stopped, the quakes died down. Were the earthquakes and the pumping related?

Government scientists decided to test this theory. They went to a dried-up oil field near the town of Rangely, Colorado. Over a period of four years, they pumped water into the old oil wells. The water penetrated deep into the earth. Whenever the water pressure got too high, many earthquakes occurred. And when water pressure dropped back down, the quakes stopped.

Scientists had found a way to turn earthquakes "on" and "off"! Eventually they hope to be able to use this procedure to prevent giant quakes. Water could be pumped into the ground where a quake was expected. The water would seep into the cracks in the surrounding rocks, causing them to slip or give, creating small tremors. Scientists hope to learn how to control these tremors. A series of small tremors might keep underground forces from building up and causing a large, damaging earthquake.

But not enough is known about this procedure. Trying it in a heavily populated area could be dangerous. If something went wrong, a deadly quake might be triggered.

Major Earthquakes of North America

In North America, earthquakes are most likely to happen in Mexico and California. The U.S. Geological Survey (USGS) has also named other major earthquake regions. They include Alaska, the Pacific Northwest, the Intermountain Belt, Hawaii, the Northeastern Region, South Carolina, and the Midcontinent Region.

A Major Quake in Mexico

The country of Mexico lies along the Ring of Fire, where four different plates act on each other, making earthquakes and volcanic eruptions very common. Mexico has five times as

Opposite:
A fissure is left by the October 1989 quake in Santa Cruz, California.

many earthquakes as California. In the last 100 years, Mexico has had 42 quakes that had a magnitude of 7.0 or more on the Richter Scale, while California has only had 5.

Mexico City: September 19, 1985

The cause of the 1985 quake was just under Mexico's Pacific Coast. The Cocos Plate had slipped under the lighter North American Plate. Great pressure built up until the Cocos Plate snapped 12 miles (19 kilometers) below the earth's surface. This released 1,000 times more energy than the nuclear bomb dropped on Hiroshima, Japan. Seismic waves moved rapidly away from the epicenter. When the quake hit Mexico City, about 230 miles (370 kilometers) to the northeast, it registered 8.1 on the Richter Scale. The vibrations were so strong that they shook tall buildings in Texas.

The quake struck at 7:17 A.M. Luckily, many businesses and schools were not yet open, otherwise, the loss of life would have been much worse. As it was, more than 7,000 died in the city. The injured numbered more than 40,000. Those left homeless have been estimated at between 50,000 to 90,000.

Mexico City actually sits on a dried-up lake bed. Building has gone on there since the time of the ancient Aztec Indians. Unfortunately, the

spongy lake bed is a poor foundation on which to build. The very strong seismic waves of this earthquake made the old lake bed wobble like a bowl full of jelly. Most of the buildings that collapsed during the quake were built on top of this lake bed.

The length of the quake also increased the damage. The tremors continued for about three minutes, which is a very long time for an earthquake. Many downtown buildings began to sway with the motion of the earthquake. If the shaking had ended quickly, there would have been little damage. But the buildings continued to shake, leaning farther over with each swaying motion until many collapsed. Hundreds of people were crushed to death between the floors of ruined apartments and hospitals.

In September 1985, a quake caused the destruction of many buildings throughout Mexico City.

△ 29

The collapse of modern buildings, like this 21-story apartment tower in downtown Mexico City, convinced city planners to revise construction codes.

Even with the massive toll in human lives and property damage, something positive did come from the Mexico City quake. Building engineers determined what they needed to do to make structures safer. For example, a new regulation required buildings in the area to be built with enough room to sway without hitting adjoining structures.

Major California Quakes

About two-thirds of earthquakes in the United States strike along faults near the Pacific Coast.

Seismologists believe the San Andreas fault first appeared on the earth's surface after the great earthquake of January 9, 1857.

The First Big Quakes

The 1857 earthquake started at Tejon Pass in the northwest corner of what is now Los Angeles County. Many buildings and large trees were knocked down. With an intensity rating of X-XI on the Mercalli Scale, it is one of the largest known early quakes. Scientists estimate that it struck with 20,000 times the energy of the nuclear bomb dropped on Hiroshima in 1945.

Fifteen years later, on March 26, 1872, another quake with an intensity of X-XI on the Mercalli Scale occurred. It hit Owens Valley, California. At 8.5 on the Richter Scale, it formed a fault 100 miles (161 kilometers) long.

The San Francisco Earthquake: April 18, 1906

At the turn of the century, many people thought that San Francisco was about as perfect as a city could be. The climate was mild, with none of the hurricanes or blizzards that hit eastern cities. The city was filled with fine restaurants and theaters, and business was booming.

Unfortunately, the city was built above the San Andreas fault. In the previous 50 years, more than 400 earthquakes had hit the area.

The fast growth of the city presented other problems. Flimsy wood houses went up almost overnight and were packed one right next to the other. The steep hills made pumping water difficult and this increased the city's fire danger. According to a report that was issued in 1906 by the National Board of Fire Underwriters, San Francisco was a firetrap. The board called the city "a catastrophe waiting to happen."

Early in the morning of April 18, the catastrophe finally struck. It was 5:12 A.M. when police officer Jesse Cook stopped at a street corner. Suddenly the street began to ripple. Sergeant Cook said, "It was as if the waves of the ocean were coming towards me, billowing as they came." The first shock lasted forty seconds. Another eyewitness said the quake made "a low, rumbling noise...as of the earth in agony." Then there was silence. Everyone waited, hoping that the quake was over.

SINGING THROUGH THE FIRE

Enrico Caruso, the famous opera singer, was performing in San Francisco in 1906. He was staying at the plush Palace Hotel when the mighty earthquake struck. Caruso sat on his bed and cried. He said later that he felt his bed rocking as though he was in a ship. Caruso was afraid that the shock of the quake had ruined his singing voice. Alfred Hertz, the conductor of the Metropolitan Opera, opened a window in Caruso's hotel room. He urged the tenor to try his voice. The sound of Caruso's singing comforted the earthquake survivors in the street below. One of them described Caruso's performance as his "bravest and best."

Later, Caruso ran into John Barrymore, a popular actor. Barrymore was wearing black tails (a fancy evening dress suit), because he had been at a party when the earthquake struck. Caruso said to him, "Mr. Barrymore, you are the only man in the world who would dress for an earthquake!"

But after only ten seconds, the earth began to shake again. Several hotels collapsed, and dozens of people were crushed. Gas and water pipes broke. Thousands rushed out into the streets. After fifteen more seconds, the quaking stopped.

Worse disaster followed. The broken gas lines leaked fuel, and splintered wood from the collapsed buildings sat like kindling, ready for a fire. Sparks shot out from broken power lines. Within moments after the quake, 50 fires had started. And because water mains had ruptured, there wasn't enough water to put out the flames. In all, 508 city blocks went up in smoke. More than 28,000 buildings were destroyed. The San Francisco Fire became the largest such blaze in the history of the world.

The San Francisco earthquake was estimated at 8.3 on the Richter Scale. It was so powerful that in only a few seconds the San Andreas fault had slipped as much as 21 feet (6 meters). More than 200,000 people were left homeless. The

The fence at this California house was displaced more than 8 feet (2 meters) during the 1906 earthquake.

exact death toll is not known. According to recent studies of old records, more than 2,000· may have perished in San Francisco alone.

Despite the earthquake's vast destruction, residents began rebuilding almost right away. By 1909, most of the buildings destroyed by the quake had been replaced with newer, stronger structures and San Francisco had the most steel-frame buildings in the United States.

The Landers Earthquake: June 28, 1992

The largest earthquake in the United States in forty years struck near Landers, California, at 4:58 A.M. It registered 7.4 on the Richter Scale and created a crack through the Mojave Desert that was 43 miles (69 kilometers) long. Three hours after the first quake, another tremor hit. It was rated 6.5 on the Richter Scale and occurred on two faults near Landers, at Big Bear Lake. These faults form two sides of a triangle with a section of the San Andreas fault. Scientists are worried that the quakes put additional pressure on the San Andreas, which could trigger a large earthquake in the Los Angeles area.

Only 1 person died, but it was especially sad. A three-year-old boy was killed by bricks that fell on him while he was sleeping. At least 77 homes were destroyed in the Landers quake, with property damage estimated at $50 million.

LOS ANGELES, CALIFORNIA: 1994

Megan and her family were sound asleep. In the morning they planned to visit Universal Studios and go on the earthquake ride. But at 4:31 A.M. on January 17, 1994, they got the ride of their lives. A quake measuring 6.6 on the Richter Scale hit the Los Angeles area.

The quake's epicenter was nearly 10 miles (16 kilometers) deep in the earth below Northridge, a suburb northwest of downtown Los Angeles. Scientists believe the quake occurred along a previously unknown branch of the Oak Ridge fault. It hit in an area where there have not been any quakes for about two hundred years. A giant plate shifted 1 to 3 feet (0.3 to 0.9 meters) upwards and actually moved the San Gabriel and Santa Monica mountains closer together.

The quake broke natural gas lines. Sparks caused towers of flame 75 feet (23 meters) high on Balboa Boulevard in Granada Hills. Water mains broke and flooded the street.

In Sherman Oaks, a young couple died when their million-dollar house slid down a hillside. Another resident, Richard Goodis, said his home was "moving like a jackhammer was going at it. Our bedroom wall tore away. I was looking at the ceiling one moment, then I was looking at the sky."

The most damage occurred near the epicenter. At least 16 residents of the Northridge Meadows Apartments died. The top stories of the building crashed down into the first floor and the garage. Resident Bryan Watson explained, "It felt like Godzilla had picked our building up, shook it, couldn't find a toy and threw it back down on the ground."

The three-level parking garage at the Northridge Fashion Center was totally destroyed. When the structure collapsed, it trapped a man working on the basement level. Giant blocks of concrete fell on the truck he was in and crushed Salvador Pena's legs. Rescuers heard his loud cries for help. They worked for seven hours to free him, using air bags and wooden blocks to lift the heavy concrete.

Because the quake struck early in the morning on Martin Luther King Day, the death toll and damage were far less than they might have been. Few cars were on the road. Most businesses and schools were not open. Even so, more than 50 people were killed and 4,500 injured. The damage totaled $30 billion and 20,000 people were left homeless.

The effects of the earthquake will be felt for some time. More than one thousand aftershocks caused further damage to weak buildings. The quake caused six major breaks in the state highways and several overpasses collapsed. Commuters had to find new, usually longer, ways to get to work.

This quake was not the expected "Big One" Californians dread. But it struck in a heavily populated area with frightening force. Ed Spies, who has lived in California since 1937, called the quake the "angriest one" he had ever felt. Barbara Bornemann lives 2 miles (3 kilometers) away from a collapsed section of the Santa Monica freeway. She said the quake hit with a loud jolt, like a bomb. It gave a wake-up call to southern California residents to be ready for "the Big One."

Alaska-Aleutian Seismic Zone

Many earthquakes have occurred in Alaska and the Aleutian Islands. This earthquake region includes Vancouver Island and the rest of British Columbia, Canada.

One of the most powerful quakes to strike this area took place on September 10, 1899. It hit Yakutat Bay, raising the shoreline 50 feet (15 meters). It measured XI on the Mercalli Scale and 8.6 on the Richter Scale.

On April 1, 1946, an earthquake registering 7.2 on the Richter Scale hit the Aleutian Islands. Damage reached a total of $25 million. The quake also caused a tsunami so powerful that it swept the Scotch Cap Lighthouse off its foundation, killing 5 men who were inside. The huge waves that battered the shore reached more than 100 feet (31 meters) in height. The waves then rushed a total of 2,300 miles (3,700 kilometers) across the Pacific Ocean to Hilo, Hawaii. There, waves up to 55 feet (17 meters) high killed 73 people.

A major quake at Lituya Bay, Alaska, struck on July 9, 1958, with an intensity of XI on the Mercalli Scale. It triggered a landslide, which, in turn, caused a tsunami nearly 200 feet (61 meters) high. But the most famous quake in the Alaska-Aleutian zone hit a well-populated area in southern Alaska, just before Easter in 1964.

The Alaska Good Friday Quake: March 27, 1964

Anchorage, Alaska, was thriving in 1964. Its population was growing rapidly and many industries, such as oil and fishing, were doing well. In fact, the city had grown too quickly. Whenever a new home or business was needed, it was simply put up—and fast. Few of the structures built were ever intended to last.

The city was perched next to Cook Inlet and was surrounded by rugged mountains. But deep within the earth, powerful, deadly forces were at work. Beneath the waters of Prince William Sound, 150 miles (241 kilometers) away, the earth's crust was under severe pressure, and was near its breaking point.

The control tower at Anchorage International Airport collapsed during the Good Friday earthquake.

It was Good Friday, the Friday right before Easter. At 5:30 that evening, people were hurrying to get home. Suddenly, at 5:36 P.M., the earth underneath Prince William Sound shifted and broke, causing a massive earthquake, which rated X on the Mercalli Scale and 8.5 on the Richter Scale.

In downtown Anchorage, the J.C. Penney Department Store was completely destroyed. The front of the building slid into the street. It crushed 1 man and killed 1 woman who was driving by in her car.

An Anchorage resident said, "People were clinging to each other, to lampposts, to buildings." Huge cracks opened in the earth, some up to 30 feet (9 meters) wide. A new six-story apartment house collapsed. Fortunately, no one was inside. A long section of the main business street, Fourth Avenue, was ripped apart. One side of the avenue dropped 11 feet (3 meters)! At Anchorage International Airport, the concrete control tower tumbled to the ground, killing an air traffic controller inside.

One of the worst-hit areas during the quake was Turnagain Heights, a very wealthy neighborhood. Modern homes were built on a cliff that overlooked Cook Inlet. The quake caused the soft clay soil to liquify. A huge landslide, 600 to 1,200 feet (183 to 366 meters) wide, slid into Cook Inlet. One family was swept away by the slide, but neighbors pulled them to safety. A 12-year-old boy, Perry Mead III, was not as lucky. He got his two younger brothers and sister out of the house. But then a gigantic crack in the earth opened up, and Perry and his 2-year-old brother fell in.

While the quake caused extensive destruction in Anchorage, only 9 people died as a result. The most damage was caused by huge tsunamis. About 120 people were drowned in the ports of Valdez and Seward. Oil that was stored near the docks at Seward exploded and created a flaming tsunami. In the end, the entire port area was destroyed.

Giant openings in the earth were created in downtown Anchorage. Before the 1964 quake, the street (shown top left) was level with the sidewalk (bottom right).

Quakes in the Pacific Northwest

In the last ten years, scientists have decided that earthquake danger in the Pacific Northwest of North America is much greater than previously believed. This region extends northward from

△ 39

Cape Mendocino in northwestern California to Vancouver Island in western Canada. The Cascade Range, a belt of volcanic peaks, runs through this region. It was created when two plates slipped under the North American plate. Seismologists believe that pressures are continuing to build up in this area and that when the pressure becomes too great, the plates will slip and a quake will occur. This is what happened in the 1964 Good Friday Alaskan quake. Some scientists fear that a similar major earthquake may hit the Pacific Northwest in the near future, causing massive destruction.

A large quake occurred in Olympia, Washington, on April 13, 1949. It was rated 7.1 on the Richter Scale and VIII on the Mercalli Scale. Eight people died and there was $25 million in damage.

Almost twenty years later, another quake hit the Seattle, Washington, area. It struck on April 29, 1965, with an intensity of VIII on the Mercalli Scale and a magnitude of 6.5 on the Richter Scale. Damage was believed to be $12.5 million and 7 people died. Today, seismologists are monitoring the Pacific Northwest region closely. They know that various indicators can give them important warning signs before a quake begins. With the proper warning, thousands of lives might possibly be saved.

Hawaiian Quakes

The Hawaiian Islands sit directly on a volcanic hot spot. This is a place in the earth's crust where a slim column of magma is continuously working its way up to the surface. Volcanic activity and earthquakes often take place simultaneously and small quakes, called volcanic earthquakes, may strike before an eruption. Sometimes, a fault fractures and a large earthquake occurs first. The shaking from the quake stirs up the magma and an eruption often follows.

The strongest known quake to hit Hawaii occurred on April 2, 1868, and had an intensity of X on the Mercalli Scale. The earthquake hit off the southern tip of the island of Hawaii and was felt 350 miles (563 kilometers) away. It also caused a tsunami that reached 60 feet (18 meters) in height and destroyed many villages.

On November 29, 1975, the island of Hawaii was hit with its largest quake since 1868. It registered 7.2 on the Richter Scale and VIII on the Mercalli. The quake caused rock to fall from the cliffs. A tsunami over 45 feet (14 meters) high swept away 21 people who were at a beach.

Intermountain Belt

In the midsection of North America is a region that is earthquake-prone. The Intermountain Belt includes Montana, Idaho, Wyoming, Utah, and Arizona. There are many mountains in this part of the country, as well as Yellowstone National Park, where there is a considerable amount of seismic activity.

Earthquakes are common in Utah's Wasatch Mountains. About 90 percent of the state's population live near these mountains. USGS surveys have been able to warn people about potential earthquakes so that those in the Wasatch region could be prepared.

A quake rated with a magnitude of 7.1 on the Richter Scale and an intensity of X on the Mercalli Scale occurred near Hebgen Lake, Montana, on August 17, 1959. The earthquake caused a landslide, which dammed the Madison River and created Earthquake Lake.

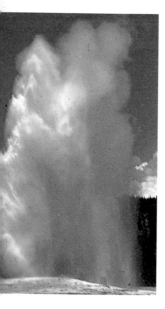

This geyser in Yellowstone National Park is an example of the extreme seismic activity in the Intermountain Belt.

The Midcontinent Region

California has been the location of the most recent and damaging earthquakes. But one of the strongest quakes in the earth's history occurred near a bend in the Mississippi River.

New Madrid, Missouri: 1811–1812

Imagine an earthquake that is strong enough to change the course of the Mississippi River. A series of such quakes hit the frontier town of New Madrid, Missouri, in the early 1800s. On December 16, 1811, the first quake hit at 2 A.M.

The ground swelled as if rolling ocean waves were passing through. Giant cracks opened in the earth, too large for horses to leap over. The quake hit with such force that it snapped thick, old trees and threw them to the ground.

Two more quakes, as well as many after-shocks, hit the area during the next few months. The third quake, on February 7, 1812, was the strongest of them all. Most of New Madrid was destroyed. Fortunately, there were few deaths, mostly because the population of the town in 1812 was small, compared to today.

The quakes were so strong that they changed the course of the Mississippi River. One steam-ship captain said that the river actually flowed upstream for a while. The river poured out over its banks and cut several new channels. In the process, it covered the town of New Madrid. Residents later rebuilt the town.

A man named Jared Brooks kept track of all of the shocks from the New Madrid quakes. He counted 1,874 all together. Brooks, who lived in Louisville, Kentucky, noticed that his pendulum clock had stopped during the first major shock. This led him to experiment with pendulums. He then built a simple seismograph to help tally the tremors. This may have been the first time anyone in the United States used a device to study earthquakes.

A Major South Carolina Earthquake

The strongest quake to hit the Atlantic Coast occurred in Charleston, South Carolina, on August 31, 1896. Scientists are not sure what caused the quake. Charleston does lie along the Atlantic Coast, but it is still more than 1,000 miles (1,609 kilometers) from the edge of the North American Plate.

Scientists who have studied reports about the quake rate it a X on the Mercalli Scale. They estimate that about 60 people were killed. The quake was so powerful that it was felt over a region of about 2 million square miles (5 million square kilometers). Cities as far away as Boston, St. Louis, and Chicago felt the shaking and the tremors. All in all, this far-reaching disaster destroyed 102 buildings and caused $4.5 billion in damage.

Charleston, South Carolina, after a powerful quake devastated the city in August 1896.

Quakes in New England and Eastern Canada

Most people think that North American quakes occur most often in California. But many earthquakes have struck New England and eastern Canada in the past 350 years. Scientists have pinpointed a 200-mile-wide (322-kilometer-wide) band that is designated a high-risk area. It stretches from Boston, Massachusetts, to Ottawa, Canada.

The first written record of a quake in New England was in 1638. William Bradford of the Plymouth Colony described a strong quake that struck in June of that year. From his descriptions, scientists have rated the quake as VIII on the Mercalli Scale.

One of the largest quakes in New England struck just before dawn on November 18, 1755. The epicenter was near Cape Ann, Massachusetts. The quake was felt from Chesapeake Bay to Nova Scotia. Brick buildings were ruined, most stone fences collapsed, and there were several landslides. It was estimated that the quake reached a X on the Mercalli Scale.

Other quakes have hit the Cape Ann area. A tremor there in 1727 was felt in Philadelphia. Another struck in 1925, a year when a series of quakes hit New England.

On Christmas Eve, 1940, a quake registering 6.0 on the Richter Scale hit New Hampshire. Seismologists gave it an intensity rating of VII on the Mercalli Scale. These are but a few of the major quakes that have rocked New England and eastern Canada in the years since people began keeping records of these events.

Predicting and Preparing for Earthquakes

In the case of many disasters, such as floods, hurricanes, or blizzards, a warning can be given. But that is not the case for earthquakes. Right now, scientists sometimes can determine where earthquakes will strike. But they are not able to pinpoint when tremors will hit.

With accurate earthquake predictions, many lives could be saved. If people knew a quake was coming, they could move to safer locations. Fewer people would be killed inside collapsing

Opposite:
A USGS technician checks one of thirteen creep meters placed at Parkfield, California, for an earthquake prediction experiment.

buildings. Natural gas and electricity could be shut off ahead of time to prevent costly fires and dangerous explosions.

Using Instruments for Prediction

Today, no one knows when a quake will hit. Just because an area hasn't had an earthquake for a long time is no guarantee that it will forever stay earthquake-free. In fact, the opposite is more likely to be true. And in a region with a history of earthquakes, a big gap between quakes may mean that a larger quake will strike when the event does finally occur. This idea is known as the seismic gap theory.

Seismologists use several different instruments to detect and measure earth movement. If these scientists notice any change in a fault's movement patterns, they are alerted to the possibility of a coming earthquake. A series of foreshocks, for example, can often hit an area before a large earthquake.

A creep meter measures the movement of the earth along a fault. The main part of this instrument consists of a wire that is stretched across a fault. The wire is attached to a post anchored in the ground at one end. The other end, which is fastened to a weight, is strung across a pulley. The weight moves up or down if either side of the fault moves.

Strain meters are placed where seismologists think the earth is most likely to spread apart. The simplest instrument has a long stainless-steel "balloon" that is cemented into the earth at a depth of about 500 feet (153 meters). As the earth spreads, the strain meter is squeezed and oil in the "balloon" is forced up the neck where it moves an expandable chamber. This movement is a direct measurement of earth strain.

These strain meters, placed along the San Andreas fault, record seismic movement. The actual instruments are buried deep in the ground and the communications equipment is on the surface. The antennas transmit the data to a USGS center via satellite.

Global Positioning Satellites (GPS) are used to measure shifts in the earth's crust. Delicate instruments in the satellites measure the position of the continents. These devices are so sensitive that they can detect how much the continents have shifted, even if the movements are as small as 1 centimeter (0.4 inches).

The U.S. Geological Survey uses instruments like these to learn more about earthquakes. The USGS is a government agency. Its western regional office is in Menlo Park, California, near San Francisco.

The USGS has set up a network of 600 seismic stations along the San Andreas fault zone in California and Nevada. A variety of instruments are used at each station. Seismometers are set up on the earth's surface. Approximately 20 strain meters have been buried deep into the ground at certain stations. A similar number of creep meters have been stretched across the faults by the USGS.

When an earthquake hits, the seismic instruments send information to a computer center. The information travels along phone lines or via microwave towers. It can come in at any time, 24 hours a day. During the day, scientists are in the center, studying the information. At night, they take turns being on call. The on-call scientist wears a pager, and if it beeps, this means an earthquake has occurred. The scientist immediately turns on a computer and evaluates the information coming in from seismic instruments.

How Risky Are Earthquakes?

What are the chances of being killed in an earthquake? Each year, there are about 100 damaging earthquakes (quakes rated 6.0 or higher on the Richter Scale). This averages out to about 1 major quake every 3 days.

Let's compare the chances of being in a deadly earthquake to other risks. About 300 out of every 1 million Americans are killed in car accidents every year. Fewer than 1 person per million die in fires or tornadoes. The risk of death from an earthquake is even lower.

Detecting Earthquakes

It seems easy to tell when and where an earthquake strikes. It simply requires noticing when the ground starts moving. But some quakes are so small that the movement may not be felt. Deciding what a quake's size is, or where its epicenter lies, is not a simple task either.

Seismologists need to know exactly when and where a quake began before they can study its cause. Then they can learn as much as possible about earthquakes and perhaps figure out ways to predict them.

This seismogram data is the recorded movement of an earthquake in Hawaii.

One instrument that scientists use to study earthquakes is a seismograph. Seismographs record ground movements and can detect even a tiny movement that is thousands of miles (kilometers) away. A seismograph has a weight hanging from a spring or wire. When a quake strikes, the weight seems to jump up and down. But what really happens is that the earth moves—up and down and from side to side. The weight is connected to a pen, which traces the earth's movements. Lines are drawn on a moving cylinder that is covered with paper. The larger the earthquake, the larger the wavy lines. This written record is called a seismogram.

A USGS scientist uses a seismograph to study earthquake activity.

When Will the Next Big North American Quake Strike?

Seismologists expect a major quake—7.0 or 8.0 on the Richter Scale—to hit southern California by the year 2000. The damage from such an earthquake would be tremendous. The Federal Emergency Management Agency (FEMA) in Washington, D.C., provides information and help in disaster situations such as earthquakes. FEMA estimates that a quake of 7.5 magnitude in southern California would cause $69 billion in property loss. As many as 23,000 people would die and 91,000 would be injured.

Earthquakes are a part of life for Californians. But many people who live in other regions of North America may not give much thought to dealing with a quake. Yet they should. In 1983, the USGS reported to Congress that the Pacific Northwest can expect a quake as big as the 1906 San Francisco quake by the year 2083.

According to the National Center for Earthquake Engineering Research, the eastern states are unprepared for a major earthquake. The center is located at the State University of New York at Buffalo. It funds research projects in earthquake engineering—such as how to build safer buildings—and provides earthquake safety education for teachers and businesspeople. According to scientists working at the center, a

△ 53

quake with a magnitude of 6.0 on the Richter Scale has a 75 percent chance of occurring somewhere in the East in the next thirty years. The death toll would most likely be very high, because the area is heavily populated. In addition, damage is expected to be severe. Few eastern cities have earthquake-safe buildings or bridges.

What to Do During a Quake

Since earthquakes can strike almost anywhere, everyone should know what to do when one hits. The best protection against earthquakes is

IS NATURE TRYING TO TELL US SOMETHING?

Many people believe that animals can sense an earthquake before it happens. Cats have been known to run wildly in circles. Birds have refused to land on the ground. Rats and mice leave their holes. Naturalist John J. Audubon reported that his horse groaned and refused to move moments before one of the New Madrid, Missouri, quakes. The night before the San Francisco earthquake of 1906, dogs howled all night. Horses and cows snorted and kicked.

There may be other natural signs of coming quakes as well. Glowing lights have been seen in the sky. Bulges may appear in fault zones. Gases have bubbled up out of lakes. Water in deep wells sometimes turns muddy.

The Chinese tried to use natural signs to determine when quakes will strike. On February 4, 1975, China successfully predicted a large earthquake in Liaoning Province. The world hoped that the Chinese had found a way to detect coming earthquakes. Unfortunately, the system failed. A deadly quake hit near Tangshan City in July 1976. It caught the Chinese completely by surprise.

It seems that in some cases, natural signs can help predict quakes. Unfortunately, all of these signs can be caused by reasons other than earthquakes. A groaning horse, for instance, might be sick. Clearly, not enough is known to make natural signs a reliable earthquake prediction method.

to be prepared. What would you do if an earthquake hit your area today? What is the best way to stay safe? What are the best ways to protect homes and possessions from earthquake damage?

The first thing to remember during a crisis situation is to try not to panic. It is helpful to remember that earthquakes often last less than a minute. If you are inside a building, keep away from the windows. Get under the strongest structure in the room. This might be a heavy chair or table. This will help protect you from falling objects.

Contrary to advice given in previous years, it's better not to stand under a doorway during a quake. According to the National Center for Earthquake Engineering Research, doorways in stores and office buildings often become too crowded and there is a risk of being trampled. Automatic doors can also cause injuries.

As soon as the shaking stops and you can safely move, get outside. Move to an open area such as a parking lot or ball field. Stay away from buildings, trees, power lines, or anything else that might fall. If you are in school, do what your teacher tells you. Students in California have regular earthquake drills. All students must get under their desks. If the ceiling falls or glass breaks, the desks will protect them.

After a quake, no matter where you are, try to remember that there may be aftershocks that could cause more damage. Don't go exploring, especially if you are near a beach or waterfront. Remember that a tsunami may strike as a result of the quake.

Help family members and neighbors to check each other for injuries. Don't move anyone who is badly injured. Have an adult check for broken water or gas lines. If you smell gas, first open windows and then get out of the building as quickly as possible. Call the gas company from a safe location. Using the telephone in a building with a gas leak might trigger a small spark, which would cause an explosion. Don't use any matches or turn on electrical switches until you're sure there are no gas leaks.

If you live in an area where quakes have occurred, gather material for an earthquake preparedness kit. Set aside enough bottled water and canned food to last several days for each family member. Have a battery-operated radio, with spare batteries, ready. Be sure you have a working flashlight, candles, first aid supplies, and any prescription medication that you need, as well a fire extinguisher, on hand. There should also be a pre-arranged meeting spot that is chosen in the event that any family members are separated during an earthquake.

RESCUE!

When earthquakes strike, people need help. Some are trapped inside damaged buildings. Many are injured. Others have lost their homes. Imagine a large quake has just destroyed a city. The electricity is out. Some buildings are on fire, and fallen bricks and glass fill the streets. What happens next?

Many cities have disaster plans. Rescue workers and city leaders have practiced emergency drills. The Federal Emergency Management Agency (FEMA) arranges them.

Several cities also have an emergency center equipped with cellular telephones, televisions, and radios. A diesel generator can be used for power if the electricity goes out. Rescue officials head to the center as soon as an earthquake hits.

Next, inspection teams fly over the quake site in helicopters. They examine structures for damage and report back to the center. Their findings help rescue leaders decide what needs to be done first.

Sometimes hospitals are damaged or destroyed. In this case, a temporary hospital would be set up. A large area such as an airport usually makes a good location. Even

Rescuers search for earthquake victims during the 1989 quake in California.

if the runways are cracked, helicopters can usually fly in and out, transporting the injured.

Rescue workers need to search for people who might be buried in collapsed buildings. They listen for any sounds of life, such as crying, or groaning. By hand, they remove parts of the damaged building. They must move carefully to prevent injury to anyone who is trapped, and be on the lookout for further danger, such as gas leaks.

Search dogs are also used to locate trapped victims. The dogs can detect a person's scent. A dog and its handler work as a Search and Rescue (SAR) team. SAR teams bring their own food and camping gear. These volunteers may stay at a collapse site for several days.

Quite often a disastrous earthquake brings out the best in people. Neighbors share food and lodging. Doctors and nurses volunteer their time. During the World Series earthquake, Dr. James Betts helped rescue six-year-old Julio Berumen. Julio was trapped in a car crushed when the Nimitz Freeway collapsed. After several hours, Dr. Betts had to amputate Julio's right leg to set him free. At last Julio was safe!

Designing Safe Buildings

Scientists have learned that some modern buildings may look great, but they aren't safe in an earthquake. Covering high-rises with glass, for example, looks dramatic, but can be dangerous in an earthquake region. Structures built with atriums (open interior courtyards) or on top of columns are not stable in such an area.

Stronger building codes have made for safer buildings. During the 1989 World Series quake, for example, San Francisco skyscrapers swayed—but they did not fall. The safest houses have wooden frames anchored to a strong foundation. Reinforced brick and concrete are other good building materials. They all flex without breaking. Since oddly shaped buildings are not as flexible as square ones, they often are twisted off their foundations.

California lawmakers passed the Field Act after an earthquake hit Long Beach, California, in 1933 and several schools collapsed. (Since the quake struck at almost 6:00 P.M., most of the schools were empty.) This act controlled the construction of new public schools. It also set strong standards to reduce earthquake risk. The act was shown to be a success after the 1971 San Fernando earthquake. It was the same magnitude as the Long Beach quake (6.3 on the Richter Scale). However, almost all of the 500 new school buildings in the San Fernando area escaped serious damage.

Building location is also quite important. Scientists say to avoid steep slopes and loose soil where landslides may occur. In the San Francisco earthquake of 1906, many of the city's buildings collapsed because they were not built on solid rock. If a structure must be built on other than solid rock, measures should be taken in order to reinforce its foundation.

Prediction Plus Preparation

Understanding the causes and effects of earthquakes is vitally important. As the world's population continues to increase, more building will be done in areas that are at risk for earthquakes. Hopefully, in the future, scientists will find ways to prevent massive quakes. In the meantime, seismologists are focusing on prediction, and citizens are focusing on preparation. These are the only ways humanity can reduce the damage and death caused by these fierce and uncontrollable natural disasters.

Glossary

aftershock Smaller quake following a large earthquake.

continental drift Theory that continents have broken apart from one large land mass and continue to move.

core The inner region of the earth.

crust The surface layer of the earth.

epicenter The point on the earth's surface above the focus where an earthquake begins.

fault A crack in the earth's crust that shows where earthquakes have occurred.

focus The area of a fault where the sudden rupture takes place at the beginning of a quake.

foreshock A smaller quake taking place ahead of the main quake.

geologists Scientists who study the earth.

liquefaction The way in which sandy soil or loose-packed earth combines with groundwater.

magma Molten (melted) rock.

magnitude A measure of strength of a quake.

mantle The rock layer between earth's crust and core; upper part is liquid.

Mercalli Scale A scale used to measure earthquake damage.

plates Large sections of the earth's crust that lie under the continents and oceans.

Richter Scale A scale used to measure earthquake magnitude.

seismic Relating to an earthquake.

seismogram The written record of an earthquake.

seismograph An instrument that records ground movements.

seismologists Scientists who study earthquakes.

tremor The shaking of an earthquake.

tsunami Giant waves caused by seismic activity.

Further Reading

Archer, Jules. *Earthquake!* New York: Crestwood House, 1991.

House, James and Bradley Steffens. *The San Francisco Earthquake.* San Diego, CA: Lucent Books, Inc., 1989.

Knapp, Brian. *Earthquake*. Madison, NJ: Raintree Steck-Vaughn, 1990.

Lampton, Christopher. *Earthquake*. Brookfield, CT: Millbrook Press, 1991.

Newton, David E. *Earthquakes*. New York: Franklin Watts, 1993.

Poynter, Margaret. *Earthquakes: Looking for Answers.* Hillside, NJ: Enslow Publishers, 1990.

HAVE YOU EVER FACED A DISASTER?

If you have ever had to be brave enough to face an earthquake, you probably have a few exciting stories to tell! Twenty-First Century Books invites you to write us a letter and share your experiences. The letter can describe any aspect of your true story—how you felt during the disaster; what happened to you, your family, or other people in your area; or how the disaster changed your life. Please send your letter to Disaster Editor, TFCB, 115 West 18th Street, New York, NY 10011. We look forward to hearing from you!

Source Notes

Blakeslee, Sandra. "Quake Effects Felt Far Away," *The Denver Post*, June 20, 1993.

Bolt, Bruce A. *Earthquakes*. New York: W.H. Freeman and Company, 1993.

Boraiko, Allen A. "Earthquake in Mexico," *National Geographic*, Vol. 169, No. 5, May 1986, pp. 654–675.

Canby, Thomas Y. "Earthquake: Prelude to the Big One," *National Geographic*, Vol. 177, No. 5, May 1990, pp.78–105.

Dolan, Edward F., Jr. *Disaster 1906: The San Francisco Earthquake and Fire*. New York: Julian Messner, 1967.

Navarra, John Gabriel. *Earthquake*. Garden City, NY: Doubleday & Company, Inc., 1980.

Pakiser, Louis C. *Earthquakes*. Washington, D.C.: U.S. Government Printing Office, 1991.

Sullivan, Walter. "Scientists Say Ocean Floor Recycled Into Islands," *The Denver Post*, June 20, 1993.

U.S. Department of the Interior/Geological Survey. *Predicting Earthquakes Along the Major Plate Tectonic Boundaries in the Pacific*. Washington, D.C.: U.S. Government Printing Office, 1990.

_____. *Preliminary Determination of Epicenters*. Washington, D.C.: U.S. Government Printing Office, 1990.

_____. *The Severity of an Earthquake*. Washington, D.C.: U.S. Government Printing Office, 1990.

Walker, Bryce and the Editors of Time-Life Books. *Earthquake*. Alexandria, VA: Time-Life Books, 1982.

Index

Acknowledgements and Photo Credits
Cover and pages 4, 8, 11, 56: ©David Weintraub/Photo Researchers, Inc.; pp. 6, 24: UPI/Bettmann; pp. 7, 21: François Gohier/Photo Researchers, Inc.; pp. 10, 22, 30, 33, 34, 37, 39, 44, 52: United States Geological Survey; pp. 13, 26: Will and Deni McIntyre/Photo Researchers, Inc.; pp. 14, 46, 49: David Parker/Science Photo Library/Photo Researchers, Inc.; p. 29: ©Wesley Bocxe/Photo Researchers, Inc.; p. 42: ©Blackbirch Press; p. 51: Krafft/Explorer/Photo Researchers, Inc.
Art by Blackbirch Graphics, Inc.